LESSONS
IN MAGIC

A GUIDE TO MAKING
YOUR DREAMS COME
TRUE

PHILIP CARR-GOMM

Published by The Oak Tree Press 2016

PO Box 1333, Lewes, East Sussex, BN7 1DX England

Tel/Fax +44 (0)1273 470888 Email office@druidry.org

ISBN: 1903232120

ISBN-13: 978-1903232125

Deep down most of us believe in magic, because we know that sometimes - just sometimes - magic can come tumbling into our lives with a blinding flash, and suddenly there we are facing the person we're destined to fall in love with, or being offered the job we never believed we would get, or we just find ourselves walking down that same familiar street, but this time it's different - this time we've fallen in love with life: this time everything looks different, and life feels wonderful and exciting again.

Most people believe that you can't make this kind of magic occur in your life. They say you're either lucky or you're not: it either happens to you or it doesn't. But what if we *could* make magic happen? What if we could do things that actually made these types of experiences occur more often in our lives? And what if there was a book that taught this kind of magic?

Magicians give birth to dreams

Magicians learn how to fly

Magicians bring magic to people's lives

CONTENTS

Apprenticed to Magic

Lesson One:

The Arrow in the Darkness

Lesson Two:

Nourishing the Seed

Lesson Three:

Jumping off the Cliff and Finding you can Fly

Lesson Four:

The Daring Adventure

Lesson Five:

The Harvest

APPRENTICED TO MAGIC

There are moments when the soul takes wings:
what it has to remember, it remembers: what it loves, it loves still
more: what it longs for, to that it flies.
Fiona MacLeod

This book is about how to become a magician.

In the old days, and in fairy tales, if you wanted to be a magician, you had to become an apprentice to a teacher, who would test and try you for months and often years, before deciding whether to accept you for training. If you proved worthy, your teacher would then slowly reveal to you a magical understanding of life, and would show you, little by little, the ways in which you could practice magic. Then, years later, once you were an accomplished magician, you would take on an apprentice of your own, so that the knowledge and craft could be passed on to the next generation.

But we're not living in the old days. The story of the world and of humanity has moved on. We've reached a critical chapter in that story and we need to act differently now, if other chapters are to follow, and the story is to continue unfolding.

Acting differently includes learning how to do magic - how to become a magician - in a new way.

There are three kinds of magic: good, bad and ineffective. Ineffective magic comes from a lack of understanding and poor technique. It's harmless but a waste of time. Bad magic involves harming other beings. Good magic helps to bring happiness, understanding, healing and joy into the world. It is something that benefits you, and also other people and the world around you.

The art of magic taught in this book will help you to realize your dreams. But it will do more than that, because real magic, powerful magic, good magic, is concerned with serving something more than yourself, as well as yourself. Real magic helps you make a difference to the world.

When I was a child I was fascinated by the idea of magic. I didn't really know what it was, but my one desire was to become a magician. I tried to learn some tricks with a conjuring set, but I could never get them to work - I was too impatient, and soon discovered that this wasn't the kind of magic that intrigued me.

Then my father introduced me to a magician. He was an old Chief Druid, called Ross Nichols, who practiced a different kind of magic. He taught me a love for the Earth and for Nature, and he showed me how to perform the magic of the Druids, by casting circles with a wand and praying to the Spirit of Life, to the sun and moon, to the stars and the rain. That kind of magic I loved, and I became his apprentice. I also discovered the magic of love, when I fell in love for the first time, and made love for the first time. It was a magical time in the world, too, because the Beatles and the Maharishi and a thousand other people were bringing another kind of enchantment into our lives.

But then the magic faded. My Druid teacher died, I began a difficult marriage, my first child was born, and I had to settle down and work hard to earn a living. But once you've experienced magic you never forget it, and although life no longer seemed so magical, I continued my training. I read widely, studied the Kabbalah, and took a degree in psychology.

The pain of an unhappy marriage drove me into the dark cave which every magician must eventually explore. And I started a different kind of magical journey - I had a Jungian analysis, and trained as a psychotherapist. As I did this, I discovered that the magic of psychotherapy was related to the magic I had learned and experienced with my Druid teacher.

A turning point occurred one morning when he appeared to me in a meditation and inspired me with the idea of teaching magic in a new way. He said "I taught you in the old way. You were apprenticed to me for years. But how many people can learn in that way? Just a handful. We need to start teaching differently. The magical temple is the world now. Life, and all the people, books and challenges we meet during our lives are our teachers now. Let's start to share our magical knowledge with many people!"

From that moment my life changed in the most extraordinary way. I began to compile a course that would teach people how to lead magical lives by combining the wisdom of the Druids with the understanding of modern psychology. I found the courage to leave my marriage, and found my first love again. With her help, and with the arrival of Desk-Top Publishing technology, we began to offer the course as a distance-learning programme, and to our amazement found that we could hardly cope with the interest it generated.

Over the coming years, thousands of people took the course. I was asked to write books, give TV and radio interviews, and was invited to teach at workshop and spiritual centres all over the world. Study groups sprang up worldwide, too, and we created a website, began residential retreats, camps and gatherings in the UK, USA, Australia and New Zealand, internet discussion groups and a monthly journal.

When I ask myself why this has occurred, the answer that comes back to me is clear and simple: "Everyone wants to lead a magical life. Everyone has experienced at least some moments of magic, and would like to know how to experience more. Magic makes people happy and creative. Happy creative people bring a positive influence into the world. Showing people how to do good magic is a good thing to do."

As proof of this, I have seen, over the years, how the ideas and methods given in the course and books have inspired and empowered people to change their lives, to write books and poems, songs and music, to plant trees and woods, to start environmental, artistic and social projects, and to fall in love again with life and the world.

You can find details of the course at www.druidry.org but in this book I would like to present the work of magic to you in its simplest, most essential form. The ideas and methods given here are the result of combining two areas of study and practice: psychology and the ancient wisdom traditions. Like some chemical combination, when these two disciplines are brought together, the result is spectacular - and very powerful. The ancient wisdom traditions, like Druidry and the Kabbalah, are full of deep insights and highly effective techniques, but they are also the products of their time, and contain outmoded ideas. Psychology's understanding of the human brain, and of our psychic structure, development and functioning, can help us to understand how the ancient traditions work, and how their knowledge and techniques can be enhanced and developed. Early behavioural and materialistic psychology was unable to do this. But much of psychology, particularly since the 60's, has advanced from this partial understanding, and we can find a potent complement to magical theory and practice in these newer approaches.

By combining the insights of these new psychologies with the ideas of the ancient wisdom traditions, this book offers a training, an apprenticeship in a new art of magic - a magic that I believe is needed by the kind of world we live in today.

The lessons are deliberately brief and deceptively simple. In simplicity and clarity is the greatest depth. So much has been written about magic that is superfluous, unnecessary or misleading. The trick is not to over-explain - if you do this, the mind gets in the way.

The old wisdom traditions knew that poetry opens us to the mystery of magic, and of Life and Spirit, in a way that prose cannot. The ancient Druids had their Bards, the Sufis their mystic poets, and every religion and spirituality has its songs, stories and poems. I am deeply indebted to the poets whose contributions appear in these lessons.

In the chapters that follow you will learn how to use the two primary tools of the magician - the cauldron and the wand, the chalice and the sword, which become, in the Arthurian and Grail stories, Excalibur and the Grail. Rather than working with these as external objects, the deepest lessons come, and the magic really starts to happen, when you learn how to open to the chalice of your heart, and how to wield the sword of your mind and will.

You won't need to learn complicated rituals and spells to perform this kind of magic. The goal of this new art of magic is not to conjure spirits or create supernatural effects. Its goal is to infuse your life with a sense of purpose, meaning, mystery and wonder - to deepen your experience of love and other levels of consciousness, and to open you to the magic of being alive.

LESSON ONE

THE ARROW IN THE DARKNESS

If I was totally free I would….
If I had all the time in the world I would…..
If I had only six months to live I would…
If I couldn't possibly fail I would…
If I could follow my dream I would…
The Song of my heart tells me to….

Magic helps you to complete the sentence, to find your dream - and to live it. Sounds crazy, too much, unbelievable to some. But to others they know it's true and want to learn how. To others still they've done this already - they know magic works and they use it every day.

You want to learn this kind of magic? Step this way…

If you don't know what you want, it's unlikely you're going to get it, so the first step is to discover what you want to achieve, what you would really like to happen in your life.

If you can complete those sentences really easily - if you have a burning passion and know just what dream you want to follow, then you can skip or skim this next bit and jump to Lesson Two. But if you're still not quite sure in which direction to head, or are curious, read on…

Magic helps you to find your bliss, the secret door in your heart that will unlock who you really are, so you can become the person you've always known you were - deep down. So you can live the life you've always known you could lead.

HOW DO I FIND THE SECRET DOOR? HOW DO I GET TO KNOW, INTIMATELY, THAT SOUL INSIDE ME WHO KNOWS WHICH DIRECTION I SHOULD TAKE, WHICH DREAM I AM DREAMING ALREADY, BUT HAVE FORGOTTEN?

Here's how:

Through crying for a vision, through darkness, through seeking a way out, through abandoning all attempts to find a way out, through loss or betrayal, through crying until your heart feels it is breaking, through poetry, through prayer, through walking, through retreat and pilgrimage, through loving and loving again, through dreams, through art, through abandonment, through crossing boundaries, breaking habits, striving for integrity, turning off the TV and entering the silence, through taking a large sheet of paper, standing on it and drawing a thick black box around you - then stepping out of the box and throwing the page away.

Now it is time that gods came walking out
of lived-in Things . . .
Time that they came and knocked down every wall
inside my house. New page. Only the wind
from such a turning could be strong enough
to toss the air as a shovel tosses dirt:
a fresh-turned field of breath. O gods, gods!
who used to come so often and are still
asleep in the Things around us, who serenely
rise and at wells that we can only guess at
splash icy water on your necks and faces,
and lightly add your restedness to what seems
already filled to bursting: our full lives.
Once again let it be your morning, gods.
We keep repeating. You alone are source.
With you the world arises, and your dawn
gleams on each crack and crevice of our failure . . .

~ *Now It Is Time That Gods Came Walking Out*
by Rainer Maria Rilke translated by Stephen Mitchell

Make a list of all your failings and weaknesses - all
the reasons why you can't find your dream, why you'll
never get what you want. Leave the list a while, then
come back to it. Read it slowly and ask yourself if any of
the things you've said are actually not failings but secret
strengths - see if you can see the light of the Gods

gleaming in the cracks and crevices of who you are. Because cracks and crevices lead down into the heart...

If you think you're not attractive, listen to Frank Sinatra singing *Funny Valentine* with your heart. If you want to be a ballet dancer but have the wrong feet watch *Center Stage*. (If you want to be anything, but are told you can't, watch *Center Stage*). If you think you're not clever enough, or keep falling flat on your face, buy a set of Tarot cards and look at the image of the Fool and know that he is closest to God. If you are handicapped watch *My Left Foot*. If you think you don't have enough money or the right circumstances around you, know that it's your decisions, and not your circumstances, that determine your future. Bernard Shaw once said "People are always blaming circumstances for what they are. I don't believe in circumstances. The people who get on in this world are the people who get up and look for the circumstances they want, and if they can't find them, make them."

When you can smile at the list you've made, when you can feel at peace with any sadness or regret you may have as you look it over, when you can sense the truth in that saying of the Bible 'And the stone which has been rejected shall be the cornerstone of the temple,' throw the list away, or file it.

Then read each of the questions at the start of this chapter and finish each sentence. Don't think about it too much, just do it!

COMMENTARY

One summer I gave a workshop with Jean Houston at Stonehenge. I talked a little of the wisdom of the ancient Druids, and demonstrated how modern Druids work magically at Stonehenge. Then Jean, in a few sentences, managed to convey to us all how powerful this magic could be. She said: "Once this mighty temple was simply a dream in the minds of a few people. They made it a reality, and for thousands of years it has stood on this land to inspire and amaze the generations. This is a work of magic. This is the work of creative genius - to be so inspired that you contribute something extraordinary to the world and to future generations. They made their dream come true."

The lessons in this book help you do just that. This kind of magic is supremely natural - as natural as conceiving a child, or planting a seed and tending it as it grows. It is the art and science of bringing ideas into form, of making what is intangible tangible. It is, in essence, the creative process - but informed with spiritual understanding.

Just as a plant results from the meeting of seed and soil, and a child from the meeting of man and woman, so this kind of magic requires a meeting of our open, receptive power with our power of focus and intention. In the East these two powers are known as Yin and Yang, and in the West they have been symbolised for centuries in magical texts by the images of chalice and wand. The chalice, cup, grail or cauldron have all been used to depict our feminine, receptive ability, while the wand or sword has been used to depict our masculine, penetrative, focused ability. Their union produces new life - whether of works of art, or of children, or of dreams born on earth.

In this first lesson you work with the chalice, the cauldron of the Self. You open your heart and mind to seek those drops of inspiration that represent your deepest wishes, your purpose, your heart's desire. You try to catch a dream.

The questions, suggestions, poetry and exercise of re-thinking your failures are all designed to help you discover not what you think you want, but what your Soul wishes to achieve.

LESSON TWO

NOURISHING THE SEED

I love…
I would love to…

Tell me all the things you love doing - all of them. Now tell me all the things you'd love to do: places you'd like to visit, experiences you'd like to have, goals you'd like to achieve. Here - somewhere in your answers to these two questions - is your dream, here is the secret door of the heart that can make your life magical. The answer or answers you got to the questions of Lesson One should also appear in your answers to these two questions. If they don't, that means there is no passion yet in your dream - and if you want to fulfill your dream it needs passion. Purpose without passion is dry and lifeless.

The key to working magic is to trust in what you love. What you truly desire is the source of your power, and that source is sacred and lies in your Soul.

You do not have to be good.
You do not have to walk on your knees
for a hundred miles through the desert, repenting.
You only have to let the soft animal of your body
love what it loves.
Tell me about despair, yours, and I will tell you
mine.

Meanwhile the world goes on.
Meanwhile the sun and the clear pebbles of the rain
are moving across the landscapes,
over the prairies and the deep trees,
the mountains and the rivers.
Meanwhile the wild geese, high in the clean blue air,
are heading home again.
Whoever you are, no matter how lonely,
the world offers itself to your imagination,
calls to you like the wild geese, harsh and exciting -
over and over announcing your place
in the family of things.

~ *Wild Geese*
by Mary Oliver from her collection Dream Work

When you have discovered your passion, purpose and soul's desire, you have your dream, your bliss, as Joseph Campbell called it. He summed up his whole philosophy of the Soul's journey, after studying all the world's religions and mythologies, as "Follow your Bliss," and he said "If you follow your bliss, you put yourself on a kind of track, which has been there all the while waiting for you, and the life that you ought to be living is the one you are living... When you follow your bliss doors will open where you would not have thought there would be doors; and where there wouldn't be a door for anyone else." That's magic - doors opening, new horizons, new opportunities, new vistas, new friends.

You might like to write down the list of things you'd love to do, and keep it in your diary - or pin it up in the kitchen or office, to act as a reminder. You probably already have lists of things you **must** do, to keep on top of life's demands. Having this other list acts as a balance - and helps you to actually do some of those things you've always wanted to do.

OK - so you've got it. You know what you want to do. You are passionate about it. You want to give your best to the world. You want to make a difference. You want to paint, dance, write, love, dream, travel, laugh, cook, sing, find that gene, play that game. What next?

HOW DO I GET THERE? TELL ME HOW TO DO THE MAGIC TO MAKE IT HAPPEN!

You have to nurse the baby that's growing inside. Making magic is no different to bringing a child into the world, or planting a seed and tending the sapling that grows from that seed.

Your dream, your desire and goal, is the seed.

The greatest achievement was at first and for a time a
dream. The oak sleeps in the acorn.
The bird waits in the egg.
And in the highest vision of a soul, a waking angel stirs.
Dreams are the seedlings of realities.
James Allen

You need to nurse the dream. Don't try to give birth to it too fast. Dreams need nurturing with rumination, daydreaming, around them. They even need ignoring for a time - so they can grow and incubate in darkness. Don't keep digging the seed up to see how it's doing. Enjoy sleeping on it. Focus on something else while feeling happy and confident inside that the seed is germinating. Drink in art and music, poetry and song. Walk in the woods, talk with friends, do doodles, eat mangoes naked (as the writer Sark says).

When the time comes to nourish the seed with thought, go sideways at it. Make a collage of photos, drawings, poems, news clippings about it. Make an altar or sacred place in your house or garden with objects and images that relate to it. Read books about it. Be open to new ideas and feelings about it. Get friends to play devil's advocate. Argue passionately for it and passionately against it. Be prepared to lose the dream and find another. Not every child gets born. Some stay in Heaven and come back another day. Don't think you're always right or that you always know what's best for you or the world.

But if your passion is still there, and you want to make it happen, take the next step…

COMMENTARY

This lesson is about finding and nursing the dream, helping it grow so that one day it can be born in the world and in our lives.

As we get older we tend to get cynical and disillusioned. We had lots of dreams in our youth, but often most of them are dead by middle age.

One of the ways dreams die is that we lose heart. When we were young we had so many dreams. Sometimes the passion in our dreams - for love or fame or excitement - may have threatened to swamp us. How many stupid things we might have done to get what we wanted! But later, as we grew older, we found that some of the dreams were hollow: what's the use of putting all your heart and soul into getting money, or power, when that doesn't bring happiness? What's the use of giving your life to your spouse or your company, when after twenty years of being there every day, they dump you? So what you do is you knuckle down, get real and lose heart.

But this kind of magic - the way taught in these lessons - says that there are other dreams, deeper dreams, stronger dreams. Superficial, illusory dreams are meant to die. But in their place - if we allow them and don't dry up and turn away from our destiny - new dreams are born like flowers that grow out of the desert in the Spring.

That's why it's worth spending time cultivating your dreams, your hopes and wishes. If you feel they're dying, or that you haven't got any - that your life is all dried up - don't hold on, let the dreams die. Feel and see the parched land around you, and then feel it aching for rain. This is your life yearning for passion, for soul, for depth, for meaning.

Spend time in the country, by a lake or river, or by the sea. When the sun shines on the water, and through the leaves of the trees - this is what you want your life to feel like. You want the gold, the green and the blue of this landscape around you. You want your life to feel like this wide open sky, these green hills, the sunshine on the water.

Feel the rain coming to your desert now. The flowers will come soon too - the seeds that have lain in the sand a long time will be germinated by the rain.

As the flowers grow in your desert, you're not sure it can be called a desert any more. It's beautiful. It's real. It's your life.

Here's a way to help you catch dreams and cultivate them:

Make three headings on a piece of paper: Having, Doing, Being. Then list under each heading your hopes and wishes. Under Having, list all the things you want: all the things you'd like to possess or have in your life, like a beautiful home, a fabulous garden, a higher income. Under Doing, list all the things you'd like to do: run for President, paint a picture, visit the world. Under Being, list all the states of Being you'd like to experience: peace, joy, pleasure, happiness, and so on.

Straight away you've got a bunch of dreams to work on. But don't make the mistake that most people do, which is to focus on the Having dreams, and then get on to the Doing dreams later, and finally - if there's time - the Being dreams. Everyone thinks that you've got to have stuff first, before you can do what you want to do, and only then can you get around to feeling the way you really want to feel - happy and fulfilled. Magic works in the opposite direction! Magic says: 'Focus on Being first. Seek contentment, fulfilment, inspiration, amazement and wonder first. Then focus on doing what you love, doing what you truly want to do in the world. Then you'll probably find you don't even need to spend time on trying to get 'things' - because they'll come to you anyway. The money, circumstances, situations, will arise and it will be easy for you to get the things you need.'

The key to working magic is to trust in what you love.

LESSON THREE

JUMPING OFF THE CLIFF
AND
FINDING YOU CAN FLY

Be practical - expect miracles.
James McCay

Once you take this next step you won't be able to control the outcome. If you're sure you really want to achieve your dream, go ahead. If you're not sure, don't worry - if it's not meant to be, it won't work. Most things don't always work - cars, coffee machines, people. And magic is just like everything else. Sometimes you plant a seed and it doesn't grow. But if you know what you're doing, if you plant the right seed in the right place, then most likely it'll grow. If you're sure you want the dream, and if it's in your best interests, and in the best interests of the world around you, the magic probably WILL work.

Magic says: 'The world is not at all what it appears to be. Every solid object is made of whirling atoms. Everything is in movement - has colour, has sound. Nothing dies. Everything changes. There are Beings, potencies, powers, love infinite and in so many forms you would melt with ecstasy if you could know them all. You can call these Guardian Angels, Extra-Terrestrial Intelligencies, Spirits, or whatever you like. Magic knows that you have friends everywhere, that the Universe is conspiring to help you fulfill your dream, that blossoming, flowering and radiating your best is what you were always meant to do, and that life and Spirit and all these Beings around you are ready to help you - at any time.

All you have to do is ask.

All you have to do is ask.

IS IT THAT EASY?

Remember when a friend, or someone you love, turned to you one day in anguish and asked for your help? And you found out that they had been struggling for months or years with this problem. And you said: "Why didn't you ask me sooner? Why didn't you tell me earlier?" You would have helped them right from the beginning. You comforted them, you reassured them, and you helped in any way you could. But you were powerless to help until they asked you.

Magic says that life works like that too. All the help you need is available - all you have to do is ask. 'Ask and you shall receive.' That is the value of prayer - of going beyond the Self to ask for what is best for you - not for what you want in the everyday sense - but for what is best for your life and Soul - for your flourishing on Earth.

If you ask for what you want, rather than what you need at the deepest level of your Being, you might still get it, but it may well surprise and disappoint you. I knew a woman who prayed for more time and she got it - she was fired from her job the next day. I heard of another woman who prayed for money, and she got it from the life insurance policy of her husband who died soon after. To get the best, and funniest education in the dangers of asking for what you want, rather than for what you truly need, see the movie *Bedazzled* with Peter Cook and Dudley Moore.

To avoid such problems, rather than asking for specifics, like a new lover, car or house, ask that your life may unfold in the best possible way - ask that if your dream is in your best interests, that it may come to be.

Prayer is one way of asking. But there are other ways too. Try walking into a bookshop, asking God, Spirit, Goddess, your Guardian Angel, to give you some advice, some inspiration. Then just pick up a book at random, open it and read the sentences that your eyes fall upon. The more effortlessly you do this, the less you use your mind to guide your hand, the more effective it will be. Once you've tried this a few times, and experienced the way in which you can often be given exactly the right advice, at exactly the right time, you will start to realize that something more than chance is happening here. **You've got friends! You just can't see them yet, that's all!**

Over the years I (and many others I have talked to) have found this process so powerful and sometimes so uncanny that I have no doubt in my mind that the Universe is conspiring to help me - and anyone else who cares to ask.

O our father, the Sky, hear us

    and make us strong.

O our mother, the Earth, hear us

    and give us support.

O Spirit of the East,

    send us your Wisdom.

O Spirit of the South,

    may we tread your path of life.

O Spirit of the West,

    may we always be ready for the long
    journey.

O Spirit of the North, purify us

    with your cleansing winds.

Sioux prayer

In many traditions, including that of ancient Egypt and of the Druids, you asked while casting an offering into sacred pools or wells. That's why we still have wishing wells - they have their origin in our distant past when we threw silver or gold into the water while asking the Goddess for healing or inspiration, or for our dreams to come true.

Asking is a form of surrender. A way of humility. A way of recognizing in your heart that you are not alone, that you do not have all the answers. It is an invitation of the heart. An invitation for something new to come into your life. It calls upon the very real presence of Spirit, of other powers and forces beyond you, who are there to help you.

All you need to do is ask.

COMMENTARY

In this lesson, you say a prayer, you wish upon a star, you offer up your cauldron, the chalice of your dreams, for the blessing of the sun and moon, inviting the help of friends in other realms, in the Spiritual World. Sometimes, to your utter amazement, this is enough, and your dream comes true. But it is more likely that you will also have to do some work: 'God helps those who help themselves.' In which case it's time to reach for your wand of will-power, intention, focus.

LESSON FOUR

THE DARING ADVENTURE

You are never given a wish without also being given the power to make it come true. You may have to work for it, however.
Richard Bach

Sometimes, just asking is enough. I could fill a book with stories from people who have asked and who have received. Miracles do happen. But sometimes you might need to do a little work to help them come into your life. This lesson describes the work involved.

If your dream hasn't landed ready-formed in your lap after following Lesson Three, ask yourself these questions and begin to write down all the steps you think you will need to take in order to realize your dream:

NOW WHAT DO I NEED TO DO, TO MAKE IT HAPPEN? WHAT STEPS DO I NEED TO TAKE? WHAT CAN I DO TODAY?

Don't say "This isn't magic - this is common-sense!" People who lead magical lives follow this process all the time - this is the way to make things happen in your life. If you find yourself skipping this lesson ask yourself why. If you want a magical life, if you want things to happen, you will have to do some work. If you want a magic wand, you will have to earn the right to own one.

Life is either a daring adventure or nothing.
Helen Keller

To begin the adventure you must take some time to plan it. Either start from your goal and work backwards to the present moment, or start from now and write down the steps you will need to take - up until the final step of actually achieving your goal. Don't worry about the exact order of the steps, you can get that right later. Just start writing down all the things you will need to do in order to achieve your goal first, then arrange the sequence later. **If you feel there are any blocks or obstacles to achieving your goal, write these down and then turn them into steps.** In other words if you want to be a guitarist but don't have the money to buy a guitar, turn the obstacle of not having money into the step of having to save or make enough money to get one.

So take plenty of time, and write down all the steps you think you need to take to achieve your goal.

Now that you have a list of steps that you need to take, make sure that you include a first step towards your goal that can be done right now. However small it is, think of the first step you can make today, so that you have actually begun to realize your dream, actually begun to put your action plan into effect. Let's take a very simple down-to-earth example. Suppose your goal is to own a car. At the moment such a goal may seem impossible. You may have no money and no driver's licence. What could you possibly do today that would move you one step closer to your dream? You could do two things. You could google or phone a Driving School for details of their fees, and you could phone a car dealer and ask them to send you a brochure on the car of your dreams. If your goal is to travel to India and spend a year there writing a book, your first step might be a call to the Indian Tourist Office for information, a request for a prospectus from a writing school, or a visit to the library to borrow a book on travel to India. However apparently impossible your goal is, there are one or more steps you can take today to start making your dream a reality.

It is so easy to procrastinate, to put things to one side, to delay things or tell yourself it just isn't possible. But if you write down such a list as your Action Plan and make the first steps things you can do right away, you set the process in motion and give yourself a far greater chance of actually achieving your goal.

A fundamental premise of magic is that Knowledge is Power. And it may well be that your first steps will be towards gaining more knowledge about your goal, or one of the steps towards your goal. This knowledge will give you the power, and suggest to you the means by which you can take the next steps forward.

Remember always the impulse behind your doing this. It is your vision. Your heart's song. Your becoming.

I cross an open field of stones, all shaped like hearts.
And say to the rocks;
"This one shall break,
And this hold the rain,
And this one be still
And this other crumple
And its grains of sand shall mark my passage."

Beat.   Beat.   Beat.
The power of the earth is moving.

We are made of Godstuff.
The explosion of stars, particles of Light.
The Goddess is with us.
Her secrets writ only in the scrolls of our hearts.
The law of creation,
of death,
and change -
Inscribed in the blood and seed of our love.

In the beginning
And at the end -
The book is opened
And we see in life what we are asked to
REMEMBER.
We veil ourselves in the worlds of illusion.

We learn how to forget . . .

What is the secret name of your soul?
From where do you get your power?
Do you know magic?
Can you offer the name of your soul
And bring yourself back to light?
Can you create life for yourself from yourself?
From the light of your works,
Do you know who you are?

Not a perfect soul,
I am a soul perfecting.
Not a human being.
I am a human becoming.

~ *Selections from Awakening Osiris*
by Normandi Ellis

If you haven't already done so, think of
something you can do now, today, that will be the first
step towards your objective.

By now you're almost ready to start taking that
first step. Remember that you may not have all the steps
in your Action Plan written down yet, because they will
only become apparent as you start following the plan.
The person who wanted to travel to India might have left

out the step of having vaccinations for example, but he or she would have discovered that step on taking the earlier step of reading travel information about India. So don't worry if you feel that not all the steps are written down.

The next thing to do, if you haven't done it already, is to jot against each step a number, starting with 1 for the first step. As you do this, you may want to rearrange the sequence.

You should now keep a copy of your final plan in your diary, or you may even want to make a chart or poster of your Action Plan to pin on the wall. Some people like to do this - others don't. It's not essential, but if you like the idea, get a large sheet of paper and spend some time drawing up your Plan. You could draw it like a flow chart, or like a flight of steps leading to your goal. You could paste photos or pictures of your goal at the top. Or you could use a spiral design with your dream at the centre. As you achieve each step, you can mark this in some way, and as you discover new steps you can add these in. And if you find you develop a different dream as you start to follow this chart, your picture will start to look really interesting as you create a new path that turns away from its original objective and moves towards something new. Taking this journey is going to be just as much fun as actually achieving your goal.

All you need to do is consistently review your Action Plan and make sure you are working towards the next step. One of these may take you years to achieve. Your ambition might be to become a psychologist for example. A major step will be taking a University degree, and that will take three or four years.

So if a step takes a long time, don't be concerned. For others, an early stage in their plan might be to sort their finances out, and save some money before taking the next step. Again, this could take a number of years to get out of debt and build up sufficient savings for the next step, which might be further training or travel for example. The value of the Action Plan is that it helps you to keep the end in mind. It makes sure you don't get lost on the way.

As you work towards realizing your dream, you will be using and developing a power that is central to the practice of magic - the power of Intention. This power manifests in the ability to focus your life and your consciousness. Focus is the magic wand of the magician. (People who know only a little about magic think the wand is an external object of power. No! The wand symbolizes an internal ability of the magician.) If you do not have the will to carry out the instructions in this lesson, it is unlikely you will have the focus required to do magic. As you work on the ideas of this Lesson, you

might like to write 'Intention & Focus' at the top of your list to remind you to keep on track.

But in addition to developing the power of intention and focus, you need to develop the ability to relax and let go, and be open. If you only focus on achieving your goals, you'll always be living for the future. You also need to enjoy life and live in the present.

So to realize your dream you need to often let go of all concerns about the future, so that you can really open yourself to the wonders and joys of living your life right now. **Because, in reality, you have achieved your dream already.** Linear time is an illusion - necessary and useful - but an illusion nevertheless at the level of Spirit and Soul. That is why Ken Keyes can ask: "How soon will you realize that the only thing you don't have is the direct experience that there is nothing you need that you don't have?"

COMMENTARY

In this lesson you pick up the wand, and carefully and deliberately plunge it into the cauldron and stir the mixture. This is the effort required to bring the elixir to perfection. The magical work is then done. You may now drink the potion and begin walking in the direction of your dream.

You have received your inspiration, you have nurtured and elaborated it, and now you can begin to manifest it in the world. A lot of people give up at this point. It requires effort and work. Studies of people who lead magical, creative lives - self-actualised people as psychology calls them - show that they are able to use both their cauldrons and their wands - their abilities to be both open and focused. They can daydream, and search for inspiration for days on end in relaxation and laughter. But once they have their inspiration, their dream, they get to work and focus with all their hearts and minds on realizing it in the world.

This lesson charts the steps you need to take to give birth to your dream in the world. In physical birth, this stage is known as parturition and is usually the most painful stage. Likewise with our own magical and creative efforts, we can often experience extreme discomfort during this phase: and this can extend from sensations of physical discomfort to ones of emotional and psychological resistance. (How much resistance did you experience to carrying out the steps outlined in this Lesson?)

A common saying is that genius or creativity involves 'one percent inspiration and ninety-nine percent perspiration' and this is certainly the perspiration phase. This is also the phase where many of us come unstuck. We are able to prepare ourselves - to take courses, to read 'how-to' books and to gather our materials together. We are sometimes able to feel inspired, and to have good and original ideas. We are then easily able to 'let go' and sleep on things for a while. But when it comes to actually 'delivering' - when it comes to finally taking those steps we need to take to complete the process, we are filled with dread. "I'm far too busy," "I'm no good at it anyway," "Others can do it better than me," "I'll never succeed" - all these thoughts come to mind, and instead of creating what we want, we stop short and don't allow the process to reach fruition.

Here are some techniques for avoiding this failure to carry out this final phase:

1   Defer judgement. It is vital that you make a decision at the beginning not to judge what you are cooking up until later. A critical judgemental stance towards what you are doing during the early stages is fatal. Be generous with yourself and make no attempt to evaluate what you are doing as you do it. If you find that despite this, you are still being judgemental, try telling yourself that you know it's not perfect, and that you will go back over it later to improve it.

2   Don't go for premature closure. This means you must not think you know the whole picture, or have all the answers. Allow whatever you are doing to grow 'out of itself' - even though you are guiding it. This will

allow things to emerge that you hadn't suspected existed. This can also mean that you should not try to complete what you are doing too quickly - it needs the right time in which to fully emerge.

3 Don't let feelings of poor self-worth stop you. Most of us have a voice inside which sometimes says: "I'm no good as whatever-it-is. So-and-so can write/sing/dance/cook etc. much better than I ever can." Or it says "Who am I to start this new venture/ open this restaurant/ dress agency etc.? There are thousands of restaurants/dress agencies/books/paintings already." Or "Who do I think I am, to be able to sort out my problems when I've never succeeded before". Listen to these thoughts (because trying to silence them can prove difficult) but don't become attached to them. Just let them float away and then carry on working.

Everyone has thoughts like this from time to time, but the successful person knows that even if their personal contribution to the world is less perfect, less wonderful, less extraordinary than others' might be, it is still unique and valuable and worthwhile because it is their own best effort - and that is what counts, not whether they will become famous or rich overnight, or whether they have surpassed the most accomplished restauranteur/actor/artist or whatever. You too should be aiming for your **personal best**, not **the** best, or someone else's idea of what is best.

41

4 Don't be afraid of making mistakes or failing. The fear of failure stops many people from trying to be more creative in their lives. But truly creative people have discovered a great secret: that there's no such thing as failure - only learning. To become accomplished in something we must learn. One of the best ways to learn is by making mistakes. As James Joyce pointed out: "Mistakes are the portals of discovery."

So as you work through the steps in this lesson don't worry about making mistakes, about getting it wrong, about whether or not you'll be able to carry out all of your plan. Don't do it too fast, and don't judge yourself harshly.

The secret is perseverance. That book of Chinese wisdom, the I Ching, constantly reminds us that 'perseverance furthers' .

The big question is whether you are going to be able to say a hearty yes to your adventure.
Joseph Campbell

LESSON FIVE

THE HARVEST

With my dream come true I can soar
It makes me feel like…
Now I know that…
I'm home

Magic is a way to help you soar, to make your dream come true, to really achieve all that you aspire to. When this kind of magic happens, it's as if you've always known life could be this way - that you could feel this good.

In Lesson One you found the inspiration - like an arrow in the darkness your spirit ranged the night, and in the depths you found the seed, the idea, the impulse, the longing.

In Lesson Two you nursed this inspiration in your belly, your heart, your mind.

In Lesson Three you asked for help, for the best to happen, for the magic to work, for blessings on this dream that you are nourishing in your soul.

In Lesson Four you were ready to give birth, and you started bringing your dream into being - one step at a time.

It may take a while for your dream to be fully manifest. Those first steps you've taken may require time and effort. But treasure these efforts for they are the beginning of your new life. If you have trouble giving enough time to your dream, know this: if you are always trying to find time, it will constantly fly from you. Instead **make** time - don't look for it.

And as your dream slowly slips into your life like a newborn child, remember to nurture it, to protect it from the gaze of others for a while - until it is strong.

Failte romhat a bhradain bhig
a chaith an bhroin le confadh saoil.
Cabhairm orm bheith mar abhainn
dod chursa om chom go saile i gcein.

Scaoil do racht is ol go faioch.
Suigh uaim suan. I gconradh ciche
sufad siar o lub do bheoil
gean le tal aris go buioch.

Failte romhat a bhradain suain
dhein lanlinn chiunin i sruth mo shaoil.
Ar sheol do chuuisle airim ceol
na nUile dom sheoladh fein.

How I welcome you, little salmon
who leapt the womb, impatient to commence life.
I undertake to be a river to you
as you follow your course from the haven of
my belly to far distant seas.

Let yourself go, and drink of your fill.
Suck sleep from me. By the terms of the breast-
contract
I'll suck back from your puckered lips
love, with which I'll suckle another time, and for that
I'm grateful.

How I welcome you, salmon of sleep
who made a tranquil pool in my life-stream.
In the rhythm of your heart-beat
I hear the music of the Heavens,
and it guides my way.

~ *Silence (Ciúnas)*
by Biddy Jenkinson
Translated from the Irish by Pádraigín Riggs

Once your dream is fully grown - once you are truly
living it, and giving it to the world, then the second kind
of magic happens - AUTOMATICALLY! The first kind
of magic is Doing Magic, the second kind is Magical

Things Happening to You: things like synchronicity - the effortless appearance in your life of people, events, experiences, love, friendship, new horizons - at just the right time. Magical days and nights. Everything turns out more perfectly than you plan it.

If you want magical things to happen to you, you need to start by doing magic. To get, you need to give first. Getting is the harvest. Giving is the sowing. Jesus said 'As ye sow, so shall ye reap,' and several thousand years earlier in the Egyptian Book of the Dead, the god Thoth said 'Truth is the harvest scythe. What is sown - love or anger or bitterness - that shall be your bread. The corn is no better than its seed, then let what you plant be good.' That's why just doing a spell out of a book without doing any work, without planting, without giving of your self, is unlikely to succeed.

When you live your dream, when you give the best of yourself, when you start to lead the life you've always known you could be living, it's as if you release waves of positive energy into the world that ripple out and touch other sources of positive energy, that send their waves flowing back to you. This is the magical Law of Resonance: that what you give out comes back to you - sometimes tenfold, sometimes a hundredfold.

WHAT IF MY DREAM IS JUST FOR ME? I DON'T WANT TO BE A MOTHER THERESA OR A NELSON MANDELA, I JUST WANT TO BE A GREAT COOK, DANCER, LOVER, GARDENER, PARENT, FRIEND!

The road to hell is paved with good intentions - just focusing on doing good can turn you into a do-gooder, and a pain in the butt. Paradoxically, to give your best to the world, the trick is to focus not on the world, but on your own dream, your own passion:

Don't ask yourself what the world needs.
Ask yourself what makes you come alive, and go do that,
because what the world needs is people who have come alive.
Howard Thurman

You don't have to earn your right to be here - to be alive. You are meant to be on this earth, and you will give of your best to the world if you allow yourself to be who you really are, to follow your passion, to fulfill your dreams, to soar - to come alive.

Better by far a person who is true to themselves, who loves what they do, and loves others for what they do, than someone who is striving only to do good, while repressing or denying their own needs and desires.

The world needs all kinds of people - some will work in medicine, or for the relief of poverty, others in art or science, while others still may not work in a conventional way at all, but may simply be fully who they are, in their own special way.

The magic lies in finding your own unique genius, your own unique way - your Bliss.

Then all you need to do is follow it. These Lessons in Magic are here to remind you - to help you hear the dream of your Soul, to help you nurture it, and to help you give birth to it, step by step.

Magicians give birth to dreams. Magicians learn how to fly. Magicians bring magic to people's lives.

THE POEMS

~ *Now It Is Time That Gods Came Walking Out*
by Rainer Maria Rilke translated by Stephen Mitchell
from 'The Selected Poetry of Rainer Maria Rilke' Picador
Classics 1987.

~ *Wild Geese*
by Mary Oliver from her collection 'Dream Work', Grove
Press, 1984.

~ Selections from *Awakening Osiris : A New Translation of the
Egyptian Book of the Dead*
by Normandi Ellis, Phanes Press, 2009.

~ *Silence (Ciúnas)*
by Biddy Jenkinson translated from the Irish by Pádraigín
Riggs, from 'An Crann Faoi Bhláth: Contemporary Irish
Poetry with Verse Translations', Wolfhound Press Dublin
1989.

Bedazzled, Center Stage, My Left Foot, My Funny Valentine can all
be watched or heard on Youtube.

If you liked *Lessons in Magic*, you might also like the training course in Druidry at www.druidry.org and

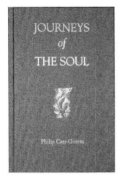

Journeys of the Soul
The Life & Legacy of a Druid Chief

In this book I tell the story of the old Chief Druid's life - Ross Nichols - mentioned at the beginning of this book. Included in this biography are selections of his poems, letters, travel diaries, watercolours and drawings.

You can buy a signed copy of the book from the store at www.druidry.org

DruidCraft
The Magic of Wicca and Druidry

This book draws on the traditions of scholarship, storytelling, magical craft and seasonal celebration of both Druids and Wiccans, to offer inspiration, teachings, rituals, and magical techniques that can help you access your innate powers of creativity, intuition and healing.

Available as an audiobook from audible.com, a paperback or ebook from Amazon, or as a signed copy from the store at www.druidry.org

SACRED NATURE HEALING MEDITATIONS

Four meditations to support
deep rest and healing:
Clothed with Flowers – a
journey to the healing world
of the Ovates and Druids,
*The Healing Island of Moy
Mell* – a journey to the Land
of Honey,

Drawing from the Well – to
help you take a brief healing catnap,
Healing Sleep – to help you go to sleep and stay asleep.
In each of these meditations the Divine Proportion is used
to convey a deep sense of harmony and healing.
The language of Nature can be glimpsed in the Divine
Proportion, also known as the Golden Mean, which is found
in the human body, in DNA, in the spirals of shells, the
geometry of crystals and the veins of leaves. It can be found
in brain wave cycles, in our skeletons, and in the branching
of our veins and nerves. The Golden Mean has been used
for centuries by artists, sculptors, architects, and composers
to produce aesthetically pleasing and harmonious creations.
In these meditations, the soundtracks have been
engineered with the Golden Mean, and it has been used in
the creation of the music.

Download the album from iTunes or Amazon

Printed in Great Britain
by Amazon

22185493R00037